Pebble® Plus

Cycles of Nature

Day and Night

by Jaclyn Jaycox

PEBBLE
a capstone imprint

Pebble Plus is published by Pebble, an imprint of Capstone.
1710 Roe Crest Drive
North Mankato, Minnesota 56003
www.capstonepub.com

Library of Congress Cataloging-in-Publication Data is available on the Library of Congress website.
ISBN: 978-1-9771-1278-1 (reinforced library binding)
ISBN: 978-1-9771-1772-4 (paperback)
ISBN: 978-1-9771-1279-8 (eBook PDF)

Summary: The sun shines bright during the day, but why can't you see it at night? Follow the patterns of the sun and Earth to learn what causes day and night.

Image Credits
Shutterstock: Aphelleon, 11, djgis, (sun) Cover, fotohunter, 15, lukaszsokol, 21, Ricardo Reitmeyer, 19, Siberian Art, 9, sripfoto, (night) Cover, Thomas Wong, 13, Tish1, 17, Toluk, (circles) design element throughout, Volodymyr Goinyk, 7, Yuganov Konstantin, 5

Editorial Credits
Editor: Alesha Sullivan; Designer: Charmaine Whitman;
Media Researcher: Morgan Walters; Production Specialist: Katy LaVigne

Note to Parents and Teachers

The Cycles of Nature set supports the national science standards related to patterns in the natural world. This book describes and illustrates day and night. The images support early readers in understanding the text. The repetition of words and phrases helps early readers learn new words. This book also introduces early readers to subject-specific vocabulary words, which are defined in the Glossary section. Early readers may need assistance to read some words and to use the Table of Contents, Glossary, Read More, Internet Sites, Critical Thinking Questions, and Index sections of the book.

Printed and bound in China.
2493

Table of Contents

The Moon and Sun

At night, the moon glows in the dark sky. When you wake in the morning, the sun is shining bright. What causes day and night?

From Day to Night

Earth is slowly spinning. It takes 24 hours to turn all the way around. This makes one day and one night.

The sun reaches half of the Earth at a time. When one half of the Earth faces the sun, it is daytime. When it faces away, it is nighttime.

Our Spinning Planet

As Earth spins, it is also moving around the sun. It takes 365 days to make one trip around the sun. This is one year.

The moon moves around the Earth. It takes about 27 days. You are probably used to seeing the moon at night. But sometimes you can see it during the day.

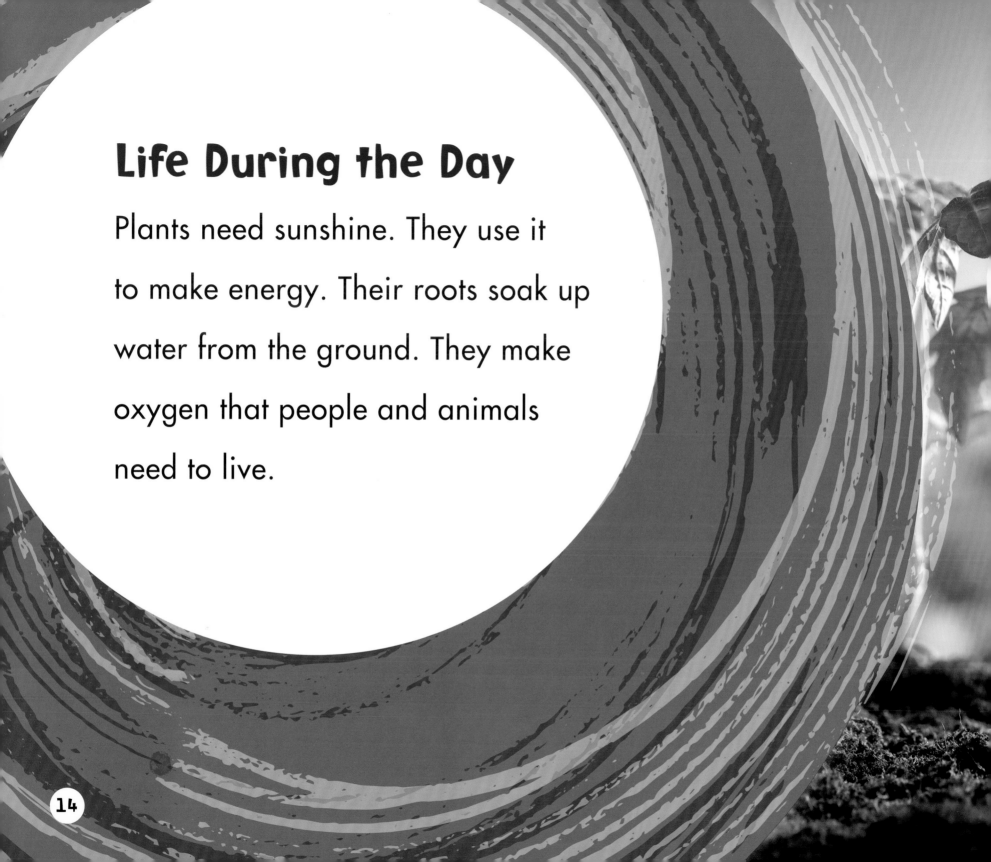

Life During the Day

Plants need sunshine. They use it to make energy. Their roots soak up water from the ground. They make oxygen that people and animals need to live.

Many animals are awake all day. They hunt and eat in the daylight. They sleep at night. These animals include squirrels, bees, lizards, and elephants.

Life During the Night

Some animals wake when the sun goes down. They can see well in the dark. They hunt for food at night. These animals include owls, bats, and tigers.

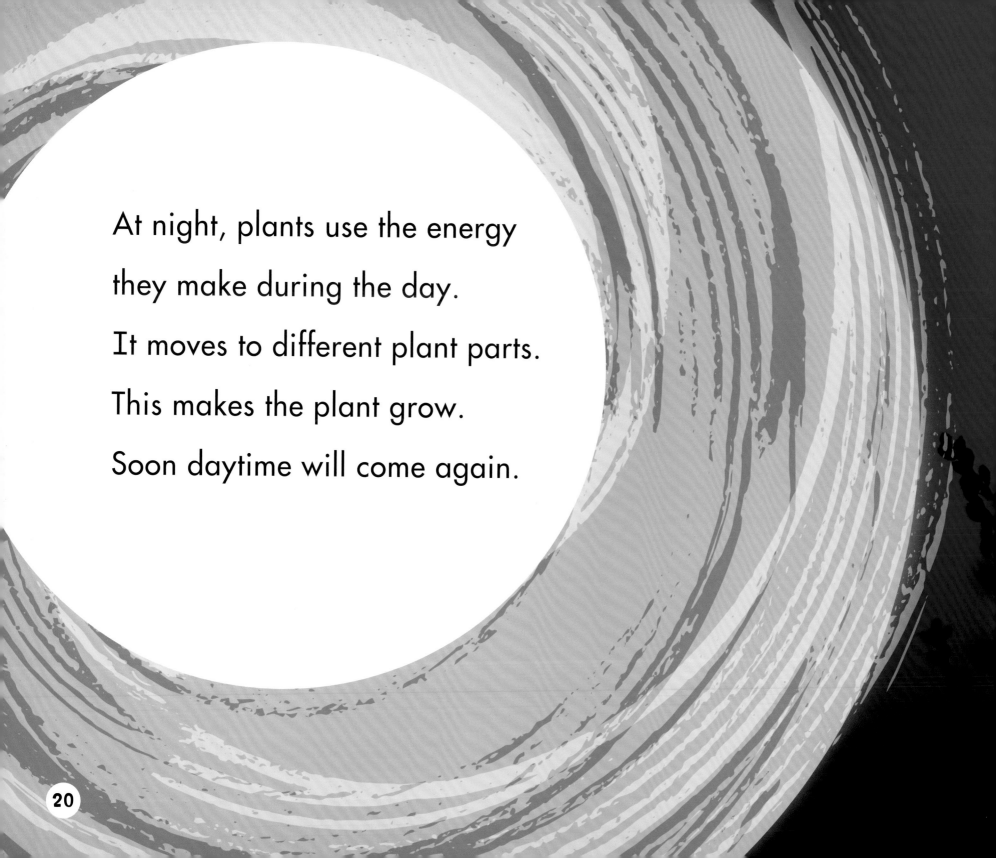

At night, plants use the energy
they make during the day.
It moves to different plant parts.
This makes the plant grow.
Soon daytime will come again.

Glossary

day—the time when your part of Earth faces the sun and the sky is light

energy—the strength to do things

moon—an object in space that moves around Earth; its light is a reflection from the sun

night—the time when your part of Earth is turned away from the sun and the sky is dark

oxygen—a colorless gas that people and animals breathe; humans and animals need oxygen to live

root—the part of a plant that grows under the ground and takes in water

soak—to draw in or absorb

Read More

Evans, Shira. *Day and Night*. Washington, D.C.: National Geographic, 2016.

Lang, Diane. *Daytime, Nighttime, All Through the Year*. Nevada City, CA: Dawn Publications, 2017.

Rustad, Martha E.H. *The Sun*. North Mankato, MN: Capstone Press, 2016.

Internet Sites

ChildFun: Day and Night Activities & Fun Ideas for Kids
http://www.childfun.com/themes/world/day-and-night/

DK Find Out!: Day and Night
https://www.dkfindout.com/us/space/solar-system/day-and-night/

ESA Kids: Day, Night, and the Seasons
https://www.esa.int/kids/en/Multimedia/Paxi_animations/English/Day_night_and_the_seasons

Critical Thinking Questions

1. How do you think animals that are hunted at night might stay safe?

2. How do you think your life might change if Earth took much longer to spin in a full circle?

Index